Dogs

English Springer Spaniels

by Jody Sullivan Rake

Consulting Editor: Gail Saunders-Smith, PhD

Consultant: Jennifer Zablotny, DVM
Member, American Veterinary Medical Association

Capstone
press

Mankato, Minnesota

Pebble Books are published by Capstone Press,
151 Good Counsel Drive, P.O. Box 669, Mankato, Minnesota 56002.
www.capstonepress.com

1 2 3 4 5 6 12 11 10 09 08 07

Library of Congress Cataloging-in-Publication Data
Rake, Jody Sullivan.
    English springer spaniels / By Jody Sullivan Rake.
    p. cm.—(Pebble Books. Dogs)
    Summary: "Summary: Simple text and photographs introduce the English
springer spaniel breed, its growth from puppy to adult, and pet care information"
—Provided by publisher.
    Includes bibliographical references and index.
    ISBN-13: 978-0-7368-6744-3 (hardcover)
    ISBN-10: 0-7368-6744-9 (hardcover)
    1. English springer spaniels—Juvenile literature. I. Title. II. Series.
SF429.E7R35 2007
636.752'4—dc22   2006028390

Note to Parents and Teachers

The Dogs set supports national science standards related to life
science. This book describes and illustrates English springer
spaniels. The images support early readers in understanding
the text. The repetition of words and phrases helps early readers
learn new words. This book also introduces early readers to
subject-specific vocabulary words, which are defined in the
Glossary section. Early readers may need assistance to read some
words and to use the Table of Contents, Glossary, Read More,
Internet Sites, and Index sections of the book.

Table of Contents

Loyal, Loveable Dogs

English springer spaniels are loyal dogs.
They make good pets.

English springer spaniels
are fast runners.
They help hunters
fetch birds.

From Puppy to Adult

Springer spaniel puppies are playful and friendly. They have lots of energy.

Springer spaniel puppies
learn to play fetch.
They also like to
play with kids.

Adult springer spaniels
are not too big
or too small.
They are almost as tall
as a fire hydrant.

Springer Spaniel Care

Springer spaniels
have long, silky hair.
Owners need to brush
the hair every day.

English springer spaniels
need water all day long.
They need food
two times a day.
Owners should not
feed them too much.

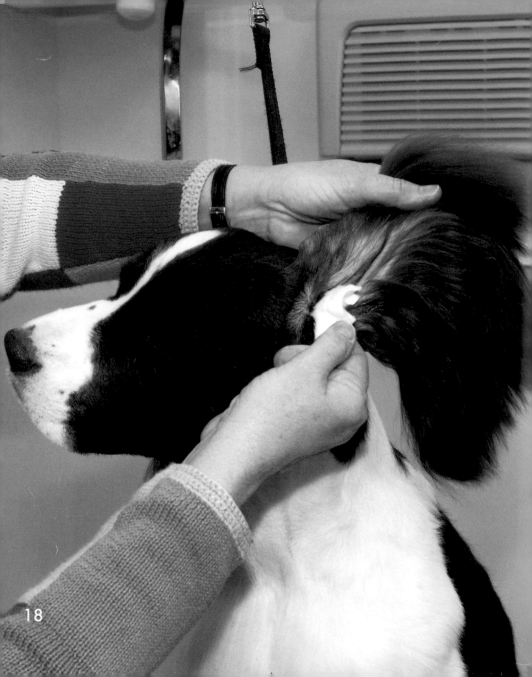

Springer spaniels
have long, floppy ears
that get dirty easily.
Owners should clean
their dogs' ears
every other day.

English springer spaniels can live in any kind of home. They like to go for walks every day.

Glossary

energy—the strength to do active things without getting tired

fetch—to go after something and bring it back

hunter—a person who searches for and shoots an animal for food or sport; English springer spaniels fetch birds such as ducks and pheasants for hunters.

loyal—faithful to a person; English springer spaniels are very loyal to their owners.

silky—very soft and smooth; English springer spaniels have silky hair.

trim—to cut small pieces off; owners trim the hair on the heads and backs of English springer spaniels to keep it short.

Read More

Furstinger, Nancy. *Springer Spaniels.* Dogs. Edina, Minn.: Abdo, 2006.

Stone, Lynn M. *English Springer Spaniel.* Eye to Eye with Dogs. Vero Beach, Fla.: Rourke, 2007.

Internet Sites

FactHound offers a safe, fun way to find Internet sites related to this book. All of the sites on FactHound have been researched by our staff.

Here's how:

1. Visit *www.facthound.com*

2. Choose your grade level.

3. Type in this book ID **0736867449** for age-appropriate sites. You may also browse subjects by clicking on letters, or by clicking on pictures and words.

4. Click on the **Fetch It** button.

FactHound will fetch the best sites for you!

Index

Word Count: 139
Grade: 1
Early-Intervention Level: 16

Editorial Credits
Mari Schuh, editor; Juliette Peters, set designer; Kyle Grenz, book designer;
    Kara Birr, photo researcher; Scott Thoms, photo editor

Photo Credits
Bruce Coleman Inc./Ernie Janes, cover
Cheryl A. Ertelt, 14, 18
Getty Images Inc./Stone/David Tipling, 6
Mark Raycroft, 10
Norvia Behling, 16; Connie Summers, 4
Photo by Fiona Green, 1, 12, 20
Unicorn Stock Photos/Gary Randall, 8